RIVERSIDE COMMUNITY COLLEGE
1916

EAGLE-VISIONED
P9-BIG-686

DATE DUE

Eagle-Visioned / Feathered Adobes

Eagle-Visioned / Feathered Adobes

RICARDO SANCHEZ

manito sojourns
& pachuco ramblings
October 4th to 24th, 1981

CINCO PUNTOS PRESS EL PASO, TEXAS

Some of these poems have previously appeared in *The Americas Review*.

 For information, write Cinco Puntos Press, 2709 Louisville, El Paso, Texas 79930; or call at 915-566-9072.

ISBN 0-938317-12-1
Library of Congress Catalog Card Number 89-085831

FIRST EDITION

■

Contents

▪

This collection
of sketches
is dedicated
to my children,

Rikárd-Sergei,
Libertad-Yvonne, &
Jacinto-Temilotzín

may you three
in your life quest
realize
that one becomes
oneself
by seeking one's history
and then accepting it
for what it was
while also realizing
that one has the right
and responsibility
to become only oneself
at whatever the cost.

years later, musings
in time/space, yet far
from where we once were
as a people in struggle...
751 Kentucky
San Anto, Tejas 78201
9th July 1986

The why of adobes & feathers:
a foreword five years later

WHEN this collection of poems and sketches was written, it was a response to the empty-scapes of arts and letters by raza in New Mexico. There were many artesans working, as well as journeyman writers, but few were those involved in questioning the very fabric of life in that enchanted land.

Sojourns in Santa Fé, as well as visits to El Paso and Albuquerque sandwiched in between moments in Northern New Mexico, produced few visions of a people in struggle. What I mostly saw were groupings of people hectically pursuing acceptance by an America deaf to the pain and hurt in barrios and rural areas where Chicanos howled a much more hurting lament than any ever penned by Ginsberg.

The same touristy mentality permeating Santa Fé can be experienced in San Antonio, for both sites dance to tourist dollars with a certain elán-anti-lo-vital.

It was depressing, such as any discordant note can be jarringly depressing. Searching for faces which once peopled the "Chicano Movement" in manitoland, I found complacency and indolence. A deep fear of repercussions was pervasive.

La Academia de la Nueva Raza had become but a flimsy shell of its former, robust declarations of activism. Its leaders had succumbed and joined those whom they had once protested. Pogo's admonition had arrived in full uniform—feathers and beads, hash pipes, tired jokes and a depressing wish for entrance into mainstream America. Railing against former compañeros was an exercise in futility.

Returning to Texas, the same conditions prevailed, and where the Academia had faltered and lost its meaning, the Guadalupe Cultural Arts Center [at that time under the auspices of Performing Artists Nucleus (PAN)] was likewise beginning to exhibit a voracious appetite for joining the American mainstream. It did so by becoming a showcase theater in the barrio catering to the well-heeled who so often enjoy moseying down to barrios and ghettos and slumming with the peasants.

The promise of the movement had been subverted, its values perverted, and its future almost cast asunder.

It is in the spirit and hope of posing questions which might lead to furthering that cause which created Chicano literature and poetry as a viable alternative to an invisible plight suffered by us [as a people] that these poems have been published.

During the heyday of the Chicano Movement, it was considered sacrilege to openly criticize leaders or fellow Chicanos. We were supposed to turn away from the graft and corruption afflicting our movement and pretend that we were truly the only honorable people in the world. Such foolishness merely crippled the movement and retarded its growth.

Having once been hustled and almost destroyed by the despotism of Anglo America in its manic drive toward total conquest of the land from Atlantic to Pacific Oceans and Canada to México, we became prey to our own sharks and charlatans.

It is now a different time, one in which we can afford to look deeper into our history and uncover the truth. The Chicano Movement produced many fine and excellent activists, some of whom died in defense of the people, i.e., Heriberto Terán, Rubén Salazar and others. It also produced many who never did gravitate to positions of power and social acceptability, but who have continued waging a struggle for the betterment of 'La Raza.'

Persons like Nephtalí de León, Dolores Huerta, Abelardo Delgado, Zarco Guerrero, Carmen de Novaís, Carlos Rosas, Bert Corona, César Chávez and the hordes of UFW, MAYA, Berets, and many others too numerous to name, brought public attention to the plight of our people.

In the space of two decades—more or less—a literature flourished, and its most valuable elements came from the streets and prison compounds. Those who began writing in academia merely wrote the nice and acceptable things demanded by tenure committees, and those works never did reach into the hearts and minds of the barrio. Though critics like Juan Bruce-Novoa continue pushing the works of academically trained poets, though Juan Rodríguez still persists in promoting the Gary Sotos of Anglicized Hispanic America, other poets will carry forth the struggle they began for the subsequent liberation of our people—a liberation which will give us the dignity we were born to enjoy, a willingness to confront our oppression, and a sensibility singing to the beauty of human diversity and cultural self-worth.

Perhaps those poets who value their words and who are willing and determined to create from their own visions a better world will ultimately topple those programs now manned by self-serving opportunists. Artists and poets should realize that assistance with strings attached is no assistance, for it is a trap which robs one of integrity and meaning. In toppling city and state-sponsored cultural programs, we might just do away with parasitic patronage. There can be no autonomy when one is forced to submit to authorities for one's livelihood, and the Guakamolee Theater in La Oreja is an example of a gutted process which could have made a difference for the people.

It is in protest to such manipulated programs, to the castrating of poetics and the de-nativizing of our cultural beings by politics and opportunism, that this selection of poems is presented.

If a poet has anything of value, it is the word which the poet lives by. In accusing programs and individuals, I stand before the reader openly. Furthermore, as a poet I wholeheartedly take full responsibility for my words. Before being a poet, before being a professor and before having a Ph.D., I am merely one man, one solitary voice who is not at all heroic...just a person with imperfections and limitations, but also a person who dreams, one who loves vision...a person hungry for that moment when our raza will have truly lived up to its promise, its beautiful potential.

No one else is responsible for the words and works in this book, thus I stand before you openly....

Ricardo Sánchez

early morning
on tejas plain,
road cuts up
north by west
through southern
voids of panhandle,
onward to little texas
eastern-ness
of Nuevo México...
4º de Octubre de 1981

sentiments hacia Belén

I. sentiments gesticulate
hacia Belén
and thence on
to Albuquerque
and Santa Fé,
arte—or is it
to be artesanía—
to be explored
within
manito expressivity,
write
something,
whether it be
a manifesto
  or a treatise,
  maybe even
  a chapbook
  or a series
  of ondas/perhaps
  a brown paper
  on disquietude

or on
an aesthetic beatitude
hammered out
by penitential
sitters on benches
carving out christ figures,
maybe a reconfigurated
Lalo Delgadoism
searching for quivira
amidst Tesuque mithopoetics,
something to do with chile verde
& other culturalist condiments,
just justify
grants and commitments made
by Yale University professor
seeking adventure
in Nuevo México, anything
that can address
the state of hispano (maybe even
chicano) arts
while eating piñones, it seemingly
cannot matter much,
when one is hired
to replace
a pretty face from new haven, ct.,
what one writes
as long as it is pleasing
or soothing
and somehow makes a point
about the intricacies
of constructions and fabrications
created neath a burnishing sun,
yes, write
that position paper
which shall explain
in quantum terminology
the exquisiteness
of culturalist expressionists
re-inventing the cultura wheel,
let that wheel turn and turn and turn,

let it roll over the brain and soul,
and, as it rolls,
do let it leave
its tracks upon
blood, history, and placid flaccidity;
we have become inured to feeling pain/truth,
let there be an abstract of it
upon the breezes amidst canyon lands,
let it be atole, chaquehue, and
sentimientos refritos,
a conceptual paper
girded by enchanted and mysterious
chants
bouncing off the sangre de cristo mountains,
it can well be an academic bit
which skims off
the chaos of the moment
or an elated sense of senselessness,
whatever,
as long as it complies
with nothing and everything
    simultaneously,
displeasing while appeasing,
a sobriquet
of maundering words,
some sibilant
and others sybaritic,
neoteric posterings
or resurrected fables,
as long as the writing reflects
a Nuevo México
that can be either real
        or feelingly imagined...

II. at long last, Belén
tomorrow Albuquerque,
but tonight Belén,
some chile verde con carne,
tortillas, and familial locutions,
much has changed, we have aged,

your world still has
the same tierra in it, mine
has become a merging
with other ways of seeing/hearing...

III. Alameda, North Valley,
Albuquerque,
your buildings
hide your mirages
Old Town had its milling tourists
  savoring
   pretensions earlier,
Bernalillo
now basks in trailer lots,
ristras hang decoratively
from your porches
while rhetorical murals
camouflage
a seedy city
no longer ours...yes,
Albuquerque, you do appear
to have some art, looked for it
within your eyes
and found shame and anomie
hiding
neath the edges of your irises...
Central and Fourth
no longer
reek of mestizos/indios,
nor does First,
only in a few crevices
do they flood the place,
damn, you've become
a gigantic taco bell,
your mild chile verde
garnishes eggs macmuffins well,
your cantos
yodel out
quasi-swiss-protestant-stinky-cheesey
  postulations,

and your cutesy adobero
    cinder-concrete-offices
    mock a past
    which has mystifyingly become
    the cultism
of The Teachings in Z. John,
newcomers
just off their boats and trains
and planes
now claim you
as their own,
Albuquerque, you are the vestiges
of born again plastic…and it does
sort of become you as you prepare
to lead New Mexico
into the 19th Century….

cool breezes
and gentle sun,
Santa Fé,
your trails
start & end
within you...
7° de Octubre de 1981

cold weather

A. cold weather
can be a blessing
if it can keep
sheening tourists away.

B. license plates
from new york
commingle
with those
from california,
utah, texas,
florida,
quebec,
and other outposts,
tourists
hustle
from indian stall
to indian stall,
original blankets
and turquoise rings
fabricated to please
are sold
on the walkways
of the governor's palace,

years of history
are later
brazenly convoluted
over drinks
at La Fonda,
chile con queso fondues,
yes, do pose
some sort of question
for tourists to muse over,
just as RC Gorman,
    Amado Peña
and a host of other
tourist pleasing
    businesspeople artists
also pose
    appeasing stances
which go well
with curtains, sofas,
and other décor...

somewhere near
d.h. lawrence
once wrote,
somewhere near
el seudo-chicano
(Jaimito Sagél)
now writes,
a lo hispánico,
we seem to inveigle
foreigners
to mimic us, or is
it possible
that their own truths
are too full of ennui
and that they must
discard theirs
and try to live ours
in order to have meaning?
Santa Fé, New Mexico
9º de Octubre de 1981

came to revisit

I. came to revisit
ancient birthplace
of my family,
came to find
the residue
of words and feelings
which once gave us
strength
and a sense of life,
have found
shards of culture,

machined kachinas,
fabricated santos
and retablos,
and a panoply of dichos
which have been
miraculously recycled;
were we ever
that simplistic
or did we buy
a media hype
in order
to sell
pieces of culture
like we did our land—
in order to survive,
so we claim—and
is this land
still enchanted?

II. humos bailan,
divujan
fantasías
sobre
una historia
fragmentada...

III. siento fríos
correr
dentro
mis pensares;
escarcha
y fastidios
se acoplan,
forniquéan—
dejan
huellas húmedas
y olorosas
como vestuarios
para un futuro
acercándoseme...

IV. es ontoño
un oktubre
chillante
y casi penumbroso,
tu luna
relumbra
por momentos
escandalizándose
inorgullosamente...

V. fabled city,
citadel of Quivira,
golden flecked dream
bathing
wanderers
from Estremadura,
Madrid,
Sevilla,
and other
castanetted/ululated
transparencies
seeking
the heart of Cíbola...

VI. Santa Fé,
I've seen your
Spanish allegations,
your vestments, pretensions,
and fractious expressions,
in between
the hispanic swaying hips
of artsy types
and the rcgormanesque displays
of mod-décor-indigenismé
hide worlds of mestizos
and native american peoples
unrecognized by you...

VII. chicos y frijoles,
solemna noche solitaria,

soledad anciana,
tierra roja
y aveces amarilla,
un norte
cual pacientemente
sonríe
sobre las tonterías
de turistas y vagamundos,
tierra acariciante,
fuerte
    y peñascosa,
pinos, montañas,
    y mesas,
poblaciones antiguas
sobreviviendo
multitudes desdichosas
    invadiendo
ruinas adobadas,
norte bello,
te reflejas
en lo sútil
de poemas
a la vez
que tus cañones y ríos
curten
la experiencia humana...

VIII. Santa Fé, Taos,
ay, nuevo méxico norteño,
tierra encantada
estás en siesta
mientras
un mundo
    anglo-sajón
intensamente busca
    formas nuevas
para
    todavía seguir
robándote
lo poquito

que no han podido robarte,
tú sonríes
recordándote
en aquellos entonces
cuando vivías
a las orillas
del mundo filistino gringo…

IX. tourists
embrace
your spanish lace,
    santa fé,
while hungered artists
pose
for a world
permeated
by images
caricaturing
the ersatz exótica
of near sylvan indo-mestizo-ness,
cute,
    bro,
this of appeasing
others
    at the expense
of our self-respect,
cuter still
our penchant
for smiling
at the right moment
or parading
in almost designer
    native garb
    in nambé movie night,
yes,
let us dance for you,
even celebrate you,
we shall please you much,
you may smack us or embrace us,
we are so damn lovable,

see us preen and shine for you,
we,
    meskin-injun
modernistic in our
    new born fetishes,
beyond the surface
    of zoot-suiting
and onward into
    native-garbing,
adoberos, jacaleros,
and little old raza people
cleaning acequias for your cameras,
we spic-n-spanishize
reality for you,
artists of all ilks
    swishing silks,
in embudo, dixon, truchas, taos,
santa fé, santo domingo, san juan,
barelas, the sawmill,
and even up to vegas & ratón,

here and there
a few artists dare to see
beyond the mockery
and in seeing
denounce everything,
yes, orlando, write your truths,
estevan sculpt your meaning,
denise indict your values, damn right,
do not please or appease
as rudy, amado, gorman, and others do,
let your art be an affirmation
which cuts
through the gelatinous morass
of the heart of a-slum,
damn, but the torturous tortuga
is a litany of basted ultimatums,
ovulate your vision
from the organ mountains in your south
to the manzanos, sandías,

sangre de cristo, and onto
the passages and cañones
of the north, cut
through the quagmires and swamps
    of stultification,
cast shadows
which criss-cross
past, present, and future,
suture
time and space
onto the filaments
of creativity, damn,
see
your tiring city
as it reposes
in vestments
which almost
sybaritically
proclaim liveliness,
realize
that Santa Fé
can be more
than
an ambulent
    cultural/anthropological
    shard or artefact,
write, paint, and sculpt
a universe beyond shidoni
    and art fests
where arts fester
and can no longer pester
    one to think...

X. floating mind,
i see
    you,
    me,
    us,
all I can be
at this moment,

my cock
strains
toward caresses
while my mind is engaged
with ideas and images
born
via breech primal screaming
idiocies,
I puff
on my own reality,
inhale hashoiled homegrown turbulations,
and smile
at a touristy multitude
amortizing
sentiment and vision,
I long
for something
never once had,
the sounds of another time
ricochet
off remembrances
while reality
is an art form
beguiling primordiality
with studious puffery,
it becomes
a shrill and hurting scream,
I
stand
only
where
I
can,
eyes
cannot look
at anyone
unless
there is a reflection
which engenders
some meaning, some purpose,

so much is a mockery,
cowboys caricature cowboys,
indians caricature indians,
hispanos caricature hispanos,
four wheel drive vehicles
    signify status/meaning
    as long as you have
    a primitive dirt road
    as a driveway
    for your overly expensive
    adobe hacienda,
I smell ristras de chile colorado
as they decorate my vision, I hunger
for hot chile
as my spittle drools over piñon nuts,
chicaspatas kachina bato, I
invert self into late night
holocaust movie, convoluted
and mentally polluted,
I roam newly created rootlessness
between chimayó and nambé
as easily as we all have
through california, utah
    arizona, tejas,
    colorado, chicago,
a human quandary, a hurting
    depersonalization,
mountains here
can be
as austere, foreboding, & alienating
as buildings in new york
or the plains of texas
    and kansas,
miles of emptiness,
buildings housing
    television addicts,
no more language
to confuse or confront us,
no, just
technological buttonizing,

from los(t) álamos
to white sands
and down
to a dead el paso
where nothing—absolutamente
    nada—pasa anymore,
just prettified
tri-cultural plays
and polite gatherings,
smoke
is
smoke
even
if
homegrown,
somehow it soothes
as it burns
through
alcoholic stupors,
    and art
is not necessarily art,
sometimes
it is a strong mural
singing hope and beauty
while giving people
a deeper sense
of their being,
other times
it is a joyous sculpture
which cauterizes
feeling and thought
into a time binding realization,
or a poem or vignette
giving form and meaning
to slanting llanos,
mostly
it is many a mediocre attempt
at hiding from oneself....

día de la raza
en Sta Fé,
no celebration,
no clarions or dances,
just a reflective utterance
before embarking
to another village, ¿Taos?,
to see weavings or retablos
or question and learn...
12° de Octubre de 1981

en lo in

i. en lo inconsciente
de andadas
por paseos de:
peralta,
santa fé trail,
gómez road,
cerrillos,
camino carlos rey
(¿o güey?),
muchas otras avenidas
miro desfiles
de mujeres mestizas,
índias,
y gavachas,
una complejidad bella,
asoleada,
y adornada
por lo encantable
y paradójico
de esta tierra manita,

un momento siento remolinos
y corajes,
el siguiente
siento cantos acariciantes…

ii. una sonrisa
ondula
por
veredas
ensedadas
a lo turístico…

iii. arte grita
sus alientos,
los turistas
recorren
vacíos intelectuales;
este museo
lleno de bullicios,
sus inquietudes y turbulencias
se agotéan
aún se enfocan
en lo rígido
de un pueblo
rústicamente
pudriéndose
sobre
el migajéo
vaciándose
de bocas
y gargantas
enturistadas;

mudos, sordos, y mediocres
hacen danza
en sus vacíos,
mentes ahorcadas
lloran idiotismos
mientras

sacerdotes enmuñecados
se bañan
en lo grotesco
de un pueblo
desnativizado,
intercambios anti-sexuales
murmuran
por callejones
donde razas desamparadas
beben
orines y comen mierdas,
Santa Fé,
sitio de porquerías
escondiendo
un pasado
basado
en la cobardía,
no se puede creer
que existió resistencia
contra los invasores,
la pestilencia atómica
vomita
sangre
y grita
sacrificio,
los bosques
lloran
genocidio,
los ríos
cantan
genocidio,
y el pueblo se estremece
en suicidio,
no se puede creer
que existió
la resistencia,
no se puede creer
que existió
un movimiento,

el tiempo
se late
en su barro existencial,
el espacio
se revuelca
en su barro existencial,
y los movimientos
se laten
en pantallas y películas,
en murallas grises
como el sudoso miedo
    del comercialismo,

dicen que los pueblos resistieron,
dicen que las gorras blancas resistieron,
dicen que el pueblo ama la tierra,
dicen que la cultural vibra aquí,
dicen tantas cosas
    en lo tiniebloso del momento
mientras
los intelectuales y artistas
broméan
con palabritas sin compromiso libertario,

y en lo chulito y pintoresco,
en los jacalitos y en los refranes,
y en lo recóndito de pueblos reprimidos
los chismes acobardan por doquier
y no se puede creer
que existió la resistencia...

iv. ruidoso claroscuro, voces
preguntan
    sobre
una literatura
    que piensan
aún ya muerta,
recuerdo
un entonces
cuando existió

un pueblo
llamado nuestro,
por un momento brevísimo
pudimos soñar
al cantarle a la luna,
    al cantarle al sol,
nuestras voces
en aquel entonces
    gritaron
con fuerza y fervor,
y el pueblo
se estremeció
apasionadamente,
sí, caray,
por un momento brevísimo
    fuímos
un pueblo
listo
para
re-crear al universo,
y ahora
somos
un gentío
contentamente
    (¡tal parece!)
vendiendo
piezas
    de mercado barato
  frente al palacio gubernamental,
la
vergüenza
ha encontrado hábito
en la mentealma
    hispánica-indígena,
y ahora preguntan
sobre una literatura
que casi nadie
ha leído....

nippy afternoon,
sipping beer,
Sidewalk Café
in Santa Fé,
12 Oct., 1981

reflections

reflections
dance about,
i think you,
    San Antonio, Texas,
city of urbanized raza
hustling other raza,
I think
of PAN O. Sha,
shyster group
of cultural vultures,
preying on sentiments
while pretending prayers
to Guadalupe
and projected plans
of theatrical possibilities,
each merely striving
to conjure
via empty promises
the means to self-promote
half-truths & funded projects,
it is
a generous feeling
to survive
alone
with only one's wits
        girding one,

to know
that I owe nothing
to ralphie & tetera
y otra plebe cool-eh-rah,
it is a high school chant
ranted over fights for monies,
integrity
is bartered o'er barrio needs,
beer is the lubricant
and mendacity the strategy,
and when the teatro has been built
the people will have to pay
in order to see caricatures
portraying raza
now controlled
by grouchy-marxists
and pseudo-artists
at the Guakamolee Cultist Arts
Theater of Absurdities & PANdejadas....

La Fonda,
drinks are tepid,
& the visages
are montaged
upon the caprices
of middle amerikan
sojourners
questing
for pop art, camp,
exotic/bewitching natives,
& pulchritudinous rendezvous...
Santa Fé, Neoteric México
12° Oktooober 1981 a.d.

assemblages

a. assemblages
of ze oldé espagne
& a wee taste
(a tad or so)
of oldie-but-goodie-méjico
commingle
in chili-con-kaysoh
and pop corn
snackeroo-botanitas,
country-western balladeer
wails out
in new englander nasality
(imported singer!)
& zee waitress wears
put-on nativeness façade
upon
her
worchester, massachusetts,
demeanor,

it's all meant to give
visiting iowans, nebraskans,
floridians, & virginny
    outlanders
a quasi-hysterical sense
of the history steeped land
where peninsular conquistadores
once sought
a fabled el dorado,
ah,
yessssss,
this is Santa Feeee,
and you damnable indians
        & mestizos
really aren't welcome
in this bistro at La Fonda
unless you act
like truly native people should,
    unobstrusive, invisible,
        and acquiescent...

b. bob dylan,
willie nelson,
charlie pride,
    freddie fender,
    & kenny rogers
  clumsy impersonations
hurl about
while
    flaccid, skin & bones
        women
   turgidly
    walk about,
giddy
    in their poses
      and reposing
        stances;
what must they think about
as they
parade

in designer jeans
  & mexican blouses?
all the while
they chatter
about
the spanish character
of the place,
they marvel
at vigas
   and ogle them
as if they were
   monstrous penises,
they squint
at their margaritas
as they sip,
   their tongues
   caress the salt
   away from their
   lower lips
   and sometimes
   they sway their hips
as they move
   to a twanging rendition
of "el rancho grandeee"
   a la ya-ni rodríguez
or freddie-the-fender,
this, too, is a strange land
for me.

c. I once thought
in salt lake,
billings, montana,
and other places
that an answer
could await me here...
I came, saw, heard,
& shall leave
without an answer,
but then
my mind

could never
conjure up
        a question here,
  for
life
has
become
    just
a moment-after-moment
    experience,
sometimes
no longer care
        to go in quest,
it is now
   more & more enjoyable
to just exist
openly
enough
to grab
    any passing experience,
taste of it,
muse about it,
and continue onward
toward
the culmination
of my life,
sometimes
i seem
to catch glimpses
of questions i would pose
to myself
and then
i would manically
run off in search
      of answers,
any answers
   would most of the time suffice,
lies were as good as truths
if they were enjoyable
or if they gave credence

to my beliefs,
that used to be fun sometimes,
other times
the answers would constrict me,
contain me, even restrain me,
they suffocated me so
that I finally had to painfully
gather up my answers
and flush out my system,

no, I am not yet cured,
once in a while
I strut out
seeking answers,
fortunately I've forgotten
  the questions
and my pockets are too full
to fill them up with inhibiting answers,
so
it has become
almost impossible
    to enjoy this place,
what with the questions
I was supposed to ask here
in order
to understand
    the nuances
    of art
    as created
    by hispanics
    & other
    mestizo
    (even chicano!)
    artists & artesans,
but as i said before,
my pockets are too full
to put any answers in them,
my questions are no longer
    in existence,
and my mindsoul

cannot envision
any question
that terribly important
that I must burden myself
    as I once did,

I'll just travel this state,
write about whatever I see,
indiscriminately do it,
it's all about the same,
people here shit
like other people do,
they pretend as well here
as we do in Texas, Alabama,
Alaska, Europe,
or in Tenochtitlán,
the spics here are just
    as greasy as anywhere else,
the injuns just as drunken,
the honkies just as materialistic
    and dehumanized,
and the niggers just as coon ass happy
    and jigga-booed,
and the japs & slants & chinks
are too few to caricature,
there are boys, girls,
    broads, dudes, a few kikes,
a wide arrangement
of human beings, each one
    playing out a role
who cares if john wayne
    was a closet queen?
or if zorro was a transvestite?
so was superfly! and tonto?
about as nutty as charlie chan!
and wonderwoman wanders around
caressing clits...so what? shit!
i know a once upon a time
dissident rooskie poet
who pretends to be hawaiian,

and he lives
in austin, texas,
and does poetry
that only
  a ukrainian
turned somoan
with a dash of
schizophrenia
can understand,
    and it is all
    the same
for him, you, me
    and huachinango
 sojourners,
he wants to be known
as
Kamehameha K. Kuzminsky
when he romps
around
poetry gigs,

and

i will not question him,
i will enjoy
some of the chaotic sounds
he makes,
but hell
it is pleasurable
at this juncture
in this stultifying place
to just sip
my drink
and
laugh
at the moment…
after all,
who can take
La Fonda & its environs
seriously?

sidewalk café
fuera
Sta Fé Council for the Arts
calle washington
near palacio del gobernador,
the world sits placidly
selling
modernistic images
of ageless relics,
plasticized turquoise
ringlets and other trinkets,
jasper, yerba de manzo,
blankets, feathers, &
ornamental idiocies... I
drink to the blasphemous
morphology of
put on nativeness, while
hybridded words swirl
upon distorted historicity...
avec-moi, queridos autores
y artistas in this
neoteric land of discoed
enchantments & condiments,
we bathe in pozole
and chorizo mestizo con papitas,
refried denizens,
zoologically illogical
in our logic...
El Pueblo de la Santa Fé,
Nueva España Mexicanada
13° Oktubre de 1981
4:00 p.m. tiempo montañoso

Compañero Orlando Romero of Nambé
you once wrote of being dropped
by an eagle near Truchas while L'il
Americano Children hydraulically became

cuando el sol ya no quema
y la mera esquema
de nuestra vitalidad deja
sus zurcos sobre nuestras
        frentes, entonces
puedo escribirte
este verso
lleno de aprecio y sonrisas,

for,

Orlando Romero, I must say
that in manito land
all orlandito children
    are given
   eagle visioned/feathered adobes

while in pachucoville
all Ricardito children
    are given
   joyous Juárez vices & putonas
    to realize,
yes,
all Orlanditos
   are given contemplative moments
   twixt acequias and peñascos,
   beaded concepts of Quivira
   chaquehuito y sopaipillas,
while
all pachuquíos are given
   atolito sin el dedo,
   un filero, una ranfla,
   un cuetero pa'l mundo,
   roach infested tenements,
   una mente muy talona,

yes, compañero,
you can view mountains, bask in nature,
fish for trout, and eat piñones,

while

we view urban women
in their mountainous undulations,
gorge on the quickness of city streets,
and dodge a panoply of cops
in their frenzied hopes
to bust or waste another one of us,

we both
hear
the plaintive cries
of la llorona
as she plies her wares
within the fear strewn labyrinths
of our ancianos' soulminds,
we feel the lash
of cruel institutions,
hear the crunching sound of hunger
ravaging our homes,
we both survive
disquieting destitution
as we exist
at the fringes
of our peoples' hopes,

writers that we are
we hurl words of fury,
some anguished, others burnished,
and all the children of our people
are given
the same turbulence
which was birthed
when our destiny—
besmirched & sullied—
was wrenched brutally
from our abuelos....

13 Okt 81

el sol

1. el sol
arde
en tardes
  enpalmadas
por visitantes
nuevainglaterraños
hormigüéan sus rayos
a la vez
que los deseos brotan
hacia caderas ondulantes,
y las quejas
    toman vacación
mientras
el poeta
   disfruta
otro momento vital…

2. enérgicamente
esculpo del barro vital
  y de sonrisas
un poemita
caluroso y alegre,
vivo aún lo que puedo
y gozo
un poco más
con cada pensamiento
lo que siento,
me estremezco,
mi pene
  se endurece,

mi sangre volcánica
conmueve al edificio
de mi alma sexualizada,
mis ojos devoran
rodillas, pies, piernas,
labios, mejillas, orejas,
ombligos, vientres, matrices,
caderas, nalgas, culos, chichis,
sobacos, codos, cabelleras,
gargantas, narices, mentes, almas,
saboreo cada clítoris con una calma
carbonizándose en las llamas
de mis anhelos,
soy sexual en mis anhelos y antojos,
mi lengua hace danza mientras mis dedos,
manos, ojos, verga, y mentealma
cantan ritmos calientes y fuertes
a esas mujeres—y son pocas—que pueden
con sus seres
crear
remolinantes visiones
en mi pensarsentir....

3. ¿quién fué
mi abuelo
más allá de lo que
pude ver
escrito en su rostro?

¿quién fué
mi padre
antes de yo conocerlo?

estoy bebiendo locuras fabricadas
en las tierras de mis antepasados,
el impulso es un chubasco
cual me lleva
hacia el buscarme
dentro historias
que nunca viví,

siento fusiles acribillarme,
    el pasado
con su condenante furia
    me enfrenta,
la tierra vomita
sus atoles prehispánicos,
lo hispánico me estruja,
lo mestizo me acomoda,
las palabras
ritméan
gestos y vaciles,
las cuestiones retumbéan:

      "¿quién eres tú
        surumato de El Paso?"

en lo recóndito
      de mi urbanidad fronteriza
  grito:

      "¡soy yo!"

          "¿qué?"

    "sencillamente soy," contesto,
y el pasado
  con su bronceado cutis
    enhuellado
  por montaña, peñasco, y chaquehue
  me habla sarcásticamente,
quiero
responder,
pero reconozco
que
la vida no es cuestión de prueba,
  entonces
le canto
    al momento
lo lleno de mi experiencia,

mi voz
se convierte
en golondrinas
que volan
hacia todas direcciones,

ay,

canta mi realidad
por calles y callejones
en el chuco,
juaritos,
los,
sanjo,
san cuilmas,
alburque,
denver,
el lago salado,
la ostión,
sacra,
la feniquera
el valle,
chicago,

ay,
canto
en las junglas nuevayorquinas
del bronx,
brooklyn,
manhattan,
lower eastside,
stoney brook,
long island,
harlem,
staten island,
riker's island,
attica,
spanish harlem/el barrio,

grito
mis cantos dentro
borracheras y putismés
de lóndres,
amsterdam,
san francisco,
mazatlán
acapulco,
méxico, d.f.,
alaska,
luxembourg,
keflavik,
northampton,
virginia,
washington, dc,
alberta, canadá, y
alabama,

y
más allá
de este momento mudo
cabalga
mi voz volante
por veredas y fantasías,

y
en
fin
vuelvo al pasado
de mis familiares
en esta tierra norteña,

siento
algo más que rencores,
el sol enhormigüéa mi piel,
oigo acentos anglosajones
resbalarse
por avenidas enadobadas,
miro turqueza, plata, y jarros,

un museo-mercado
valorizado
por lo extranjero,
mi garganta
resecada por la historia
no puede ni quiere hablar,
las palabras se me vuelven salitre,
mis pensamientos se petrifican,
y ni preguntar sobre
verdades quiero ya,
mi sombra baila
sobre
su sombra
a la vez
que mis sueños
lloran por ser más que sueños
soñando
fantasías vivibles,

se retuerce
la tierra nuevo-mexicana,
chuchupaste hierve en los sentidos,
se revuelca la toma de la historia,
la cultura se hace atole encholotado,
murciélagos se cagan en los dichos,
biscochitos de salitre enpachan
lo sentimental del ayer,
lo simple de los anhelos
en el vómito de la realidad
se mezcla
entre experiencias variadas,
y el retoño
sólo es
un viaje al claroscuro, nada fijo,
nada neto, una carcajada,
su saludo y una despedida,
del polvo a la polvadera...
a las cuatro y media de la tarde
suenan
los clarines,

se enfilan los colmillos,
y gruñen las barrigas,

a las cuatro y media de la tarde
siento
lo alejado que estoy
en este pueblo de extranjeros,
siento
la amistad de otras tierras
y bebo lo fructífero
de mis recuerdos,

sí,
a las cuatro y media de la tarde
la escarcha otoñol
corta al tiempo,
cachetea mis momentos,
y broméa con los sentimientos,

y

en ese espacio
recorro mi futuro
para abrazar mis inquietudes
cuando regrese a mi tejas…

4. es más
que un predilecto
y menos
que un regocijo sexual
el beber
cerveza tibia
en una tarde fría….

la cocina café
en Santa Fé...
18° de Octubre de 1981

residual sounds

I. residual sounds
reverberate,
last night's
    reconnoitering
into pseudo academic games
    in nambé
became
a blasé usual
        venturing
    into contrived
  nativeness
     a la anglo-sanforization;

the drinks
were customary
    Mexican beverages
 and the food
a doughy
      spaghetti,
and the discussions
   (led
     by native-garbed women
        in blonde coiffures)
were doughier....

II. orlando
danced, argued,
and later felt
(so he said)
dismayed & perhaps dismally bad
over
their
incomprehensions,
i
merely recalled
many other
encounters
where hosts
invite those
they wish
to patronize,
where one must smile just so
while saying with some contrition
that one shall not practice sedition,
oh, yes, josé,
where one must be a particularly polite
spic&span kind of ano,
a niggy, a four feathered injun
who is cutely native,
or even a clean & purty smelling bilikin
or crafty yet kind of couth cajun,
the host did patronize
if only for a scant few minutes,
and the hostess did pretend
to like our kind of folks,
the beer was cold,
you had a choice
between tecate & bohemia,
no coors or bud or even oly,
and they did like
orlando's salsa dances and his cumbias,
if only we had stated
all they wished to hear,

how dare you, orlando,
state
that our literature
has universal properties?
how dare you, orlando,
displease
those nice & patronizing people?

didn't you realize
that they invited us
that we might share
our native, savage innocence?

III. nuevo méxico,
¿será posible
    que tu norte
    se ha hecho
    tal como tu chile
    ahora se hace?
a watered-down
    and piss poor replication
of a past
            now en-tombed?
yes, santa fé,
republic
of shoddy, tourist pleasing replications,
much
has died
    and been left
to fester
    upon your features;
invaded,
    you seem to have acquiesced,
and, like the serpent,
devoured yourself
within
the brine
of self-disdain…

caressive afternoon,
I see you,
Santa Fé...
tonight
shall I write to you
and read to you
& in that way
embrace you...
a bit beyond noon,
not even gary cooper
stalks this place today,
it's not even ze
oh, kay, corral up
your cowboyish staggerers
kind of kinky moments,
it's a hotkind of day
the kind whereeverythingjust
runs together, the sweat
agglutinates one thought
to the other, can't seem
to separate feelings...
21° de Octubre de 1981

en esta tierra

I. en esta tierra
lloran sueños
los alacranes;

en esta tierra
brotan llantos,
gruñen pinos;

en esta tierra
    se atomizan
los piñones;

en esta tierra
    cascabéan
los peñascos;

en esta tierra
    se cabalgan
los anhelos;

en esta tierra
    se amparan
a los duelos;

en esta tierra
    ambuléan
las soledades;

en esta tierra
    vive hueca
nuestra historia;

en esta tierra....

II. santa fé meanderings
    create
their own
panoramas,
    multitudes
parade about,
each visage
begets
another visage,
    medicine
is another word
for pandemonium

when bewitching folks
convert
    fear
into remembrances
of dachau, buchenwald,
and the santa fé
    prison butcher shop,
words here
sound off
into franciscan friar chants,
buildings
merge
into a past
which is now
expensive chic,
and many a derelict
who once was poor
    within his/her failure
is now a bonafide success
lucratively tapping
into relics & cultural artefacts,
each
one
dressed
in
shards
& clownish
regalia,
billy d. kid, donny quixote,
yawn chisolm, bitch cassidy,
el general armijo,
padre martínez,
bishop lamy z. lamebrain,
a d(isturbed) h(ijodeputa) lawrence
folktale
taking a stroll
in a city
where every-pinche-day
is a sunday-easter/keeeesterlike-
    afternoon, finery abounds,

sights, colors, sounds,
& 3-dimensional buffoonery,
the grandest—mayhaps the only—game
in this town
which closes up its reality
at 9:00 pm
every night of the week
and twice on sundays.....

III. biting wind
cuts
into
feelings,
hands
pneumatically numb
    themselves,
cold
prances
through fingers
    remembering
warmth
      from just
    a few hours ago,
  and older recollections
    of beguiling skin
 dance
on ends of fingers,

thoughts play, transporting me
    to many places
       and warm beds, I walk
into the foaming silence
     of dirt roaded
         adobe haciendas a la plastíque,

I walk
trying to recall words
          and hopes
     of living
  within

the sun torched
    san juanero bounds
    of my ancestors
and am seared
by garish pastiches
entablados
    for preening tourists,
and
I walk
into sears & roebuck fabricated
    galleries, see prints
  upon prints
which could match
    my drapes & sofa,
if only I had drapes and sofa,
    this décor, this city
could well accommodate
a thousand taco-bell buildings,
and the tourists would all
probably feel
that they had had
authentic-genuwhine
cuisine a la mexique
        or spaans...
or at least
bien comidos pero no cogidos.

IV. stoned,
    my words
    pirouette
    upon
    mellifluous
    crevice ridden senses,
a film of lugubrious hunger
gnaws
on itself,
thighs
    and eyes
     inveigle,
fantasy beckons,

and
poetry
    enjoins me
    unto
    my own
    enjoyment
while musing
as I peruse
each woman,
    some
    are
    worthy
    of being loved
for their minds,
others
for their spirituality,
and there are those few
who
excite the world
with their hedonistic-
    let-us-be-complete-
    in-our-enjoyment-stances-
        and-walks,
many are those
who
exist
beyond
any excitement,
who only express disdain,
loneliness, fear,
and repressive sentiments
in their ugly and angry scowls,
those I cannot look at
and so leave them be....

almost evening,
about to read,
whiskey y mota
play
on my potted
senses—yes,
  cabrones, it
is wednesday
  in
Santa Fé, NM
 21st Okt 1981
  6:15 PM MST

desfiles

A. desfiles
    nalgonométricos,
aún
   casi un París
envuelto
     en trajes
        y esculturas
              de barro,
este cafecito de banqueta,
THE WASHINGTON STREET DELI,
hasta en lo frío
ambuléan
    por do quier,
visiones nalgonométricas,
todo tipo de expresión
se promulga...

B. han cambiado
bastante
las cuestiones,
ya no
retrocéan
ni tampoco
retumban,
los horizontes
son
más
serenos
al igual
que los hambres
son
más
calmados...

C. hoy ví
ojos
vacíos y dolorosos
hambrientamente
buscando
una avenida
donde la soledad
pueda ser
tan siquiera aguantable,
recordé mis ayeres
dentro lo solitario
de mi hoy
y en mis silencios
al estar acompañado
por mi bebida
sólo suspiré
al re-encontrarme...

D. recuerdo
en esta espacio
lo erótico
del ayer, aún cuando
tú te bañabas
en lo jugoso
de nuestras palabras—

¡sorprendido!—pues
    te acaricié
sobre el espaciotiempo
    de nuestra separación
y terminé
    cantándonos
un momento fragrante
    de los cuales
nos dieron aliento
    en nuestra juventud—
¡sí! todavía te quiero, mujer,
todavía....

22 october 81

beyond

beyond
the plastique
    of the moment,

there is
    song,

and realness
dancing
        is
 but a
  reflection
of
  the beauty
one can live-
        love....

la cocina café,
el chile
y el refín
cantan...
sf,nm
23 oct 81

frío suele quemar

I. frío suele quemar
a la vez
que canta
realidades norteñas...

II. Orlando,
you sit
discussing
cartesian theory
and aesthetic meanderings,
you fly
intelectualmente
into worlds
beyond acequias
and chaquehue,
all the while
your arte
is
an
artful
defense
steeped
in lo caribe
of our land...

III. más tarde
haremos danza poética
en los rincones
de la prisión,
pensamientos enculebrados
ondularán
por laberintos
permeados
por lo esquizofrénico,
murciélagos autoritarios
vampiracirán
sentimientos amargosos
mientras
el acero
gritará
su aliento desesperado
sobre
un espacio
estancado en la solapa
eternalizante
de los rechazos sociales...

early morn coffee shop,
hamburgered breakfast
and art rap, Suzanne
Jamison, you are damn
good people, and
you truly care and want
to create
a better world...am
leaving this land today,
also finally leaving
those dreams I once had
about coming to what I
felt was my home, realize
that it is merely the home
of my ancestors, my home
shall ever exist
just beyond every horizon
I encounter, I really
don't have a land that
is mine, and I might just
not even have a people
to contain me and my
soulmind's questings....
enroute to Albuquerque,
Belén, El Paso, San Antonio,
& then Austin, Tejas
24° de Octubre de 1981

nos sentamos

1. nos sentamos,
Suzanne,
sobre un almuerzo...
lo tibio del café
y lo chillante
de Santa Fé

murmuran
  una artesanía
      brutal
    y aún turística,
we discuss
precise vagaries
    & other arts,

yes, i will write
a thing or two
about
the arts i saw,
that suicidal tree print
was riotous,
the hollywood indian
at the indian art fest,
and the quasi indio things
    put out by amado buffalo peña
a la r.c. gourmet gorman,
the carvings of estéban,
the murals of guzmán,
the dramas of denise,
the filmy beauty of orating
    órale orlando,
maybe even write
about the stiltedness
    of zee rudee-anahuak-anaya,
will write
someday
about those
lovely women
doing time,
      their poetry
      was
    tantamount
to seeing flowers bleed,
pain
encrusted upon more pain,

such beauty
within
such a silencing pain,
will write a poetic sketch
    (i tell you),
algo con sentimiento
about
many of the experiences
i had with the art
at shidoni,
nambé, the library murals,
the galleries,
embudo,
the works
as they worked within my mind
and soul,
it will be
poetry,
not prose
        nor academic drivel,
it is not
that i cannot write
a treatise or an abstract
or a chapbook
or a treatment
or even a critíque,
it's just
that poetry
is the only thing
that turns me on
when
my mindsoul galavants
through
experience and reflection,
and, Suzanne,
art
was an experience for me
in this disquieting place,

for it prefaced every sentiment
as well
as it expressed
a culture and a people dispossessed,
never truly found
my people
        in the arts,
only found
        our desultory
  societal invisibility,
and it did hurt
to realize again
that hispanics in the arts
      is a fantasy in neuvo méxico
shadowy people
that we've become,
our art
      perhaps
is that survival game we play,
a tour de force
      enacted everyday,
an oral art
that's handed down
to help our young
      survive another day,
arte
is that legendary creature
hiding
amidst the sandías,
      organ mts,
and the sangre de cristo
      ranges,
it hibernates
within the villages
and plays hide & seek
in albuquerque barrios;
someday, Suzanne,
our art
might resurrect itself

and claim anew
the tierra
that we've lost,
it will be indio,
mestizo,
   and chicano,
but not hispano,
that's what
our art shall be...

2. Albuquerque,
te miras
todavía
como
una distorción
   histórica
entre
tus arenales,
tu duque
duerme
bajo murallas
del
dolor social,
y tú
festejas bullicios
anunciando
un pasado nunca vivido.

3. Juan José Peña,
your eyes
sadden
space
while your pain
saddens
time
as experience
spaces you out,
you sit,
      your words
   are tired,

they create
woven images
of tiredness/resignation,
you seem
to be retiring,
the movement
    has used you
so you state,
and now
you want
to roam about
into just
remaining in one place,
your pasture beckons, carnal,
and you seek a job
where
you can be
only juan josé,
un obrero
who no longer wants to organize
nor confront
nor hurl anger at
    a still racist world,
yes,
you say,
  "This is it. I am tired
      and now shall retire,"
that
it is time
to leave
your
Raza Unida Party behind—
    within
the chiaroscuro
of time in its spatial soup...
I hear
the creaking of your soulmind,

I see you
reaching out for anonymity,
    a rest, a respite;
you've done your thing, carnal,
and I respect you
for what you've done,
yes, Juan José,
do retire,
take off the mantle
    of leadership
you once wore
with dignity and pride,
    realize
that you have given
much of yourself
to our people's movement,
that you also have the right
to now look after your own,
that your children must also eat,
that you have the right
    to sit back and read
        your newspaper,
    in your easy chair,
    comfy slippers on,
    puffing on a pipe,
    and once in a while
regaling children and grandchildren
with the fact
that you once led
a national political party
seeking
revolution,
you have fought
until tiredness, envy,
bickering, police threats,
economic isolation, and
so many other problematic
    quandaries
have stripped you
of will, strength,

dammit, Juan José,
it is not shameful
to admit defeat
when one has fought
and sacrificed
as much as you have done,

you, at least,
realize
that you have waged a struggle
while most people
have mutely stumbled about
  fearfully,
you've struggled
and you seemingly have lost,
so go lick your wounds,
recuperate,
and then go seek
that place
wherein you can survive...
  buena suerte, compañero....

4. Nonie Tenorio,
chaotically alone,
sentenced
to exist
within
the penitentiary
of this state
forever and a day,
habitual felon
in manitoland,
you shall fast
and die
within a couple
  of months,
you state,
your eyes
solemnly
express conviction,

too old
to do that
      much damn time,
you shall fast and die
and the Santa Fé
      State Penitentiary
shall claim
your body, Nonie,
but not your mind and soul,
and
it is possible
that you shall
at long last
have a modicum
of peace
within
the grey coverlet of death,
Nonie,
    memories of you
      at UTEP
when you were a pinto at La Tuna
shall float here and there,
then when
Dr. Gardea & I
took you
to a Juárez congal
that you might
      relearn
the joys of a warm blooded woman,
it was a rare moment of camaraderie,
or that time in Albuquerque
when you showed up
with a suitcase full of turquoise,
or that .44 magnum
    with a buntline barrel,
damn, many a good time
spent by us, and now
you seriously will walk
that last mile
into a fasting death,

can't tell you to take it easy,
nor wish you
season's greetings,
nor shall I purport
to tell you what to do,
I understand
the words, the feelings,
and the ideas
motivating you,
I, too, feel
that
when one is old
and tired,
death is preferable
to a lifetime
in a prison world;
why die
    a day at a time
in the sameness,
    in that barrenness
of prison?
old convicts
    make ugly looking
        corpses,
    they really do,
and death or illness
    in prison
is a lonely/horrid
    and loveless thing.
better to die now,
go quickly
    into the grey of death!
a fasting death
    filled with fantastical imagery,
a death
    of hope filled
     hallucinations,

a two month vigilance
anticipating
death, yes,
that is precisely
    wiser
than years
    of empty hopes,
cold/cold beds,
    and tasteless food.
life
    encaged
has no humanizing message,
especially
when one realizes
that all one can look forward to
is an eternity
of todays, each day the same,
forever, ever the same;
yes, Nonie, you want to die,
like all hopeless pintos
        want to die,
I really can't blame you, bro,
        really can't....

5. Manolo, carnal,
we share
        food
            and
                drinks,
smoke a bit,
speak
orgiastically
of life,
    finally
are we becoming
brothers
    on the outskirts
        of Belén,

yes,
Nolo,
after many years,
you
ever the oldest
of the brothers
in the family,
finally
we share
ideas, motivations,
and more than words,
we drink and sing,
and plan
reunions,
vibrantly
we part,
I go on
toward
El Paso and then Austin,
you
stay on in Belén,
years ago
when
the Navy discharged you
after World War II,
you studied music/singing
at Juilliard
in the Big Apple,
sophisticated Nolo,
you were
a très chic Chicano
in a 1950's El Paso,
a city too small
    and rustic
to appreciate
a meskin
who read Whitman
    and sang
in semi-operatic tonalities,

you dressed too well,
your artist mind
was too developed
for a city
too infested
    with terse fears...

6. el paso,
southernmost city
of New Mexico,
westernmost city
of Tejas,
you recline
between nations
and feel tensions
amidst
    peoples distrusting
  each other,
all
the
while
desert visages
dance
upon sage,
sand,
  and smog filled skies,
your mountains
fear
that someday
greenery
might bloom
upon them,
and sometimes
you whitewash murals
that people
might not learn
to laugh and sing,

schizoid city,
your definition of self
cries out
in chaos
every tuesday morning
and then is silent
for the rest of the week,
your militants
roam
your alley ways,
each one wanting
to become
more than a furtive shadow
burrowing
through the bleakness
of a defeated city...
you are loved
for being a landing pad
for many a people
seeking quivira,
and you are hated
for being
an illusion
to those
who seek
meaning in
the sunsets
o'er your mountains

Glossnotes®

Regional Spanish Vocabulary and Notes on Allusions in Eagle Visioned/Feathered Adobes

compiled by M. S. Hetherington

Abbreviations

adj	adjective	*phr*	phrase
fem	feminine	*pl*	plural
fr	from	*Sp*	Spanish
i.e.	that is	*qv*	which see
interj	interjection	*v*	verb
n	noun	*var*	variant of
part	participle	*vr*	reflexive verb

Poems Cited

ANV	Alameda, North Valley	*JJP*	Juan José Peña
ass	assemblages	*Mc*	Manolo, carnal
bey	beyond	*nsS*	nos sentamos, Suzanne
bw	biting wind	*NT*	Nonie Tenorio
COR	Compañero Orlando Romero	*Orl*	Orlando
ctr	came to revisit	*qf*	¿quien fue?
cw-lp	cold weather [and] license plates	*ref*	reflections
des	desfiles	*rs*	residual sounds
eli	en lo in...	*sf*	siento fríos
ep	el paso	*SF*	Santa Fé
es	el sol	*sfm*	santa fé meanderings
fc	fabled city	*shB*	sentiments hacia Belén
fm	floating mind	*tou*	tourists
fsq	frío suele quemar		

References

Acuña *Occupied America: The Chicano's Struggle Toward Liberation.* Rodolfo Acuña. New York: Harper & Row, 1972.

Cass *Cassell's Spanish Dictionary.* New York: Funk & Wagnalls, 1968.

Cobos *A Dictionary of New Mexico and Southern Colorado Spanish.* Rubén Cobos. Santa Fé: Museum of New Mexico Press, 1983.

Galván *El diccionario del español chicano.* Roberto Galván and Richard V. Teschner. Silver Spring, MD: Institute of Modern Languages, 1975, 1977.

Porrúa *Diccionario Porrúa de la lengua español...rev. por Francisco Monterde.* 5th ed. Mexico D.F.: Porrúa, 1986.

Sánchez Ricardo Sánchez, in response to query

Glossnotes®

acoplarse *vr* *Cass:* "To become intimate *(colloquial)*" *sf*

adobero *adj* Adobe-styled *ANV*

adobero *n* Adobe-maker *pl* in *tou*

agotearse *vr* Overflow *eli*

ahorcada *adj* Strangled *pl* in *eli*

alburque Short form or nickname for Albuquerque *qf*

Amado Amado M. Peña Sánchez: "A Chicano-Tejano artist from Laredo who underwent a metamorphosis into an Indian artist from New Mexico" *tou*

ano *n* [*Sp* 'anus'] Play on words as the last three sounds of the word *hispano* *Orl*

armijo Gov. Manuel Armijo of New Mexico, who repulsed the first invasion of that land by Texans in 1841 but who capitulated in 1846 under suspicion that he accepted a bribe from Col. Stephen W. Kearney not to resist (Acuña 57-58) *sfm*

a-slum, heart of *qv* Allusion to the book *Heart of Aztlán* by Rudolfo A. Anaya and pun on the word *Aztlán, qv* *tou*

asoleada *adj* Sánchez: "Sun-burnished" *eli*

atole, atolito *n* Cobos: "corn mush or gruel" *shB*

Aztlán Chicano name for land where the Aztec peoples are said to have lived before they migrated south of the Río Grande (or Río Bravo), an area including all or most of California, Arizona, New Mexico, Colorado, and Texas, and parts of other states *tou*

barelas Barrio (ward or neighborhood) in Albuquerque *tou*

bato *n* Cobos: "guy, fellow, dude" *fm*

Belén Town in New Mexico where Sánchez visited his brother Manolo en route to Santa Fé by appointment to spend a month observing and commenting on the cultural arts there for the New Mexico Commission on the Arts. *shB*

caray *interj* Sánchez: "Damn right" in *phr "sí, caray" eli*
caribe *n* Cobos: "a kind of chili sauce made with raw red chili peppers" *fsq*
carnal *n* Cobos: "brother" *Mc*
Cíbola Legendary city with streets of gold sought by early European treasure-seekers and looters of the American continents *fc*
cogido *past part* [*coger v*] Sánchez: "Fucked" *bw*
congal *n* Galván: "Brothel, whore house; beer joint" *NT, sfm*
cool-eh-ra Pun on *Sp culera,* shitty *ref*
coraje *n* Poetic song *pl* in *eli*
cuetero *n* Sánchez: "Gun" *CO*

chaquehue *n* Cobos: "[*fr Tewa*] mush or porridge made with blue cornmeal" *shB*
chicano *n* Native U.S. citizen, usually of Mexican and native American descent, active in the movement for civil and social rights and equality, educational and economic opportunity foreword, i *et al.*
chicaspatas *n pl* Affectionate term for Mexican-Americans *fm*
chichis *n pl* (slang) Breasts, tits *es*
chillante *adj* Sánchez: "Shrill" *sf*
chimayó Town in northern New Mexico *fm*
chuchupaste *n* Cobos: "*chuchupate* [*Mex. Sp* a medicinal plant] same as *oshá* in northern N.M." *qf*

dancing *n* Allusion to Sánchez' wife Teresa, who danced professionally before their marriage *bey*
Delgado, Lalo Abelardo Delgado, longtime friend of Sánchez and with Sánchez one of the authors of a book of poetry, *Los Cuatro* (Denver, 1971) *shB*
Denise Denise Chávez, writer *tou, nsS*
dicho *n* Proverb or saying *pl* in *ctr*
divujar *v var dibujar ctr*

embudo, dixon, truchas Villages in northern New Mexico *tou;* embudo also *nsS*
encholotado *adj* Sánchez: "Americanized" *qf*
enculebrado *adj* Serpentine *pl* in *fsq*

enmuñecado *adj* Sánchez: "Pansyfied" *eli*
estancado *adj* Sánchez: "Stagnant" *fsq*
Estevan Estevan Arrellano, sculptor *tou, nsS*

feniquera Nickname for Phoenix, AZ *qf*
filero *n* Sánchez: "Shiv, switchblade" *COR*

gavacha *adj* Cobos: "Anglo-American woman; gringa" *eli*
Gorman, R. C. Navajo artist whose work attained great popularity in New Mexico *cw-lp, nsS*
gorras blancas "White caps," name and part of a costume which has its origin in the white robes and hoods of the Spanish Inquisitors, also copied by the Ku Klux Klan *eli*
Guakamolee Double pun and allusion to Guadalupe (Cultural Arts Center in San Antonio) see foreword ii *ref*
güey *var buey* 1: *n* [*Sp* 'ox'] Dumb ox (a person) 2: *adj* Cobos: "stupid" *eli*

hormigüear *v* *Porrúa:* "To have a feeling like that of ants crawling upon one's skin" *es*
huachinango Reference to 'put-on' tourist airs *ass, bd*

Jamison, Suzanne Director of the Santa Fe Council on the Arts *nsS*
juaritos Sánchez: "Nickname for Ciudad Juárez, Mexico, directly across the Río Grande from El Paso, TX" *qf*

kachina *n* Indian religious figure *fm*

lamy, bishop *sfm* see *martínez*
lawrence, d. h. Allusion to his book *Sons and Lovers* *sfm*

llorona, la Cobos: "the wailing woman [*Sp llorar*] People believe la llorona to be...a ghost that wails in the night as a sign of danger or impending death...." *COR*

manito *adj* [*Sp hermanito 'little brother'*] Native of New Mexico *shB*
Manolo Manolo R. Sánchez, oldest brother of Ricardo Sánchez *Mc*
manzanos Mountains in New Mexico *tou*

manzo *n* Medicinal herb common in northern New Mexico *COR*

martínez, padre Padre Antonio Jose Martínez of Taos resisted the policies of Bishop J. B. Lamy of Santa Fé, who was a friend of Kit Carson and other Anglo-Americans oppressive to the native residents (Acuña 65-66). *sfm*

mera *adj* Cobos: "true, real" *COR*

migajeo *n* Sánchez: "Crumminess" *eli*

movimiento *n* The Chicano movement, described in the foreword to this book *eli*

nalgonométrico *adj* Sánchez' compound composed of nalgón *(Sp* 'large buttocks') + métrico *(Sp* 'measurement') = buttocks to the nth power *pl* in *des*

nambé Town in northern New Mexico *tou, rs*

nuevainglaterranos *n pl* New Englanders *es*

oly Olympia brand beer *Orl*

ondas *n pl* Sánchez: "Happenings" *shB*

Oreja, La Sánchez: "The Ear, nickname for San Antonio because the people there hear everything that is going on" foreword, iv

Orlando Orlando Romero, head of Southwestern Collections in the New Mexico State Library at Santa Fé and author of the autobiographical novel *Nambé: The Year One.* Sánchez fashioned the structure of the poem "Compañero Orlando Romero" as an allusion to the novel. *COR, Orl, tou*

Ostión Literally, large oyster Sánchez: "Pun on the name of Austin, TX, and reference to the fishy stink of the state capitol" *qf*

pachucoville Sánchez' nickname for El Paso, TX *COR*

PAN Performing Artists Nucleus (see foreword) *ref*

PANdejadas Pun on *pendejo,* 'fool,' and allusion to *PAN* *ref*

PAN O. Sha Pun on *panocha* [Galván: "Vulva"] and allusion to *PAN, qv* *ref*

Peña, Amado *cw-lp, nsS* see Amado

Peña, Juan José One-time national chairman of La Raza Unida whom Sánchez visited while surveying the arts in Santa Fé *JJP*

Penitents The Brotherhood of Penitents, a movement formed before its members learned that Mexico had been freed from Spain *shB* see also *Gorras Blancas*

pinche *adj* Sánchez: "Damn" *sfm*

pinto *n* 1: Cobos: "Inmate in a penitentiary" 2: Sánchez: "Also a Chicano ex-convict" *pl* in *NT*

pozole *n* 1: Porrúa: "Dish made of corn and pig's head" 2: Native herb *COR*
prison butcher shop Allusion to a riot at the Santa Fé State Penitentiary *sfm*
putona *n* Sánchez: "Whorishness" *COR*

quivira Same as Cíbola, *qv* *ep, shB*

ralphie Ralph García, a founding director of *PAN, qv* *ref*
ranfla *n* Sánchez: "Hot rod" *COR*
raza *n* Sánchez: "My people; the current significance of the term comes from *La Raza Cosmica* by José Vasconcelos, first minister of public education in Mexico (1882-1959)" *ref*
rcgormanesque *adj* *SF* see *Gorman*
rechazos sociales *n phr* Sánchez: "Rejects of society, *i.e.* prisoners" *fsq*
rudee-anahuak-anaya *nsS* see *Rudy, Tortuga, ultimatums*
Rudy Rudolfo A. Anaya, New Mexico novelist *tou*

Sagel, Jaimito Sánchez: "James Sagel, a gringo writer who married a Chicana and who passes for a Chicano"; a leader of the Hispanic literati in New Mexico *ctr*
san cuilmas San Antonio A number of San Antonians who went to California served time there in San Quentin prison; when they returned home, the name San Cuilmas, a nickname for San Quentin, somehow became associated with the name of San Antonio. *qf*
sandías [*Sp sandía* 'watermelon'] Mountains near Albuquerque, so called because the setting sun colors their western cliffs watermelon red *nss, nsS*
sangre de cristo Mountains near Santa Fé, *NM* *ass*
san juanero *adj* Reference to the Tewa Indian pueblo of San Juan, where Sánchez' maternal grandmother was born *bw*
santos and retablos, fabricated *phr* Sánchez: "The commercialization of what used to be a personal and spiritual expression" (the hand carving of wood figures of saints and icons by Native Americans) *ctr*
shidoni Shidoni foundry and gallery near Santa Fé *tou, nsS*
solapa *n* Sánchez: "Isolation" *fsq*
sopaipillas *n pl* Puffy pastries, often served dusted with confectioner's sugar or with honey *COR*
spaans Dutch for 'Spanish' *bw*
spic-n-spanishize Sánchez: Pun on spick-and-span and the derogatory term "Spik" for a person of Spanish origin or one who speaks Spanish *tou*
surumato *n* [Northern New Mexico expression] Southerner *qf*

talona *adj* Sánchez: "Hustling" *COR*

Tejas Indian word for friendship and origin of the state name Texas *ep*

Teachings in Z. John Allusion to *The Teachings of Don Juan* by Carlos Castaneda *shB*

Tenochtitlán Sánchez: "Along with Tlatelolco, twin city-state and capital of the Nahuatl nation in Mexico" *bd*

Tesuque Pueblo (Indian reservation) in New Mexico *shB*

tetera Juan Tejeda *ref*

tortuga *Tortuga,* novel by Rudolfo Anaya *tou*

Tuesday morning Allusion to a series of breakfast meetings at the El Camino Restaurant in El Paso to discuss problems of the Chicano Movement and to work out solutions, meetings which later became mere social gatherings *ep*

Tuna, La Prison at Anthony, a town on the state line of Texas and New Mexico *NT*

ultimatums, basted *phr* Allusion to the novel *Bless Me, Ultima* by Rudolfo Anaya *tou*

UTEP University of Texas at El Paso *NT et al.*

Yale U. professor Juan Bruce-Novoa, now of Trinity University in San Antonio *shB*

ya-ni rodríguez Pun on the name Johnny Rodríguez (vocalist) *bd*

zoot-suiting *adj* Sánchez: "Superficial" Allusion to *Zoot Suit,* a play and film by Luis Valdez *tou*

zurcos *n* Sánchez: "Turnrow" *pl* in *COR*

■

RICARDO SANCHEZ

(b. 1941), whose father moved to El Paso in 1938 for political and economic reasons, was the first member of his maternal or paternal family to be born outside of the northern New Mexico region since the 17th century. Thus, he is a "manito" by heritage and a "pachuco" by place of birth and experience. A high school dropout, he received his Ph.D. from Union Graduate School, Antioch College, 1974. He was the only U.S. poet invited to the first meeting of the Poets of the Latin World which met at the Palace of Fine Arts in Mexico City, 1986. He and Teresa, his wife of 25 years, have three children and two grandchildren.

Photograph © by Rikárd-Sergei Sánchez.

Other Works by Ricardo Sánchez

■

Books

Selected Poems. Arte Público Press, University of Houston, Houston, TX, 1985.

Amsterdam Cantos (y poemas pistos). Place of Herons Press, Austin, TX, 1983.

Brown Bear Honey Madnesses: Alaskan Cruising Poems. Slough Press, Austin, TX, 1981.

Milhuas Blues and Gritos Norteños. Spanish-Speaking Outreach Institute, University of Wisconsin, Milwaukee, WI, 1980 & 1978.

HECHIZOspells. Chicano Studies Center/Publications Unit, University of California at Los Angeles, Los Angeles, CA, 1976.

Canto y Grito Mi Liberación/The Liberation of a Chicano Mind. Anchor Books, Doubleday & Co., Garden Çity, NY, 1973, an expanded reprint of *Canto y Grito Mi Liberación (y lloro mis desmadrazgos).* Míctla Publications, Inc., El Paso, TX, 1971.

Chapbooks

Bertrand & the Mehkqoverse: A XicAno Filmic Nuance. Slough Press, Austin, TX, 1989.

Perdido: A Barrio Story. Published by Rob Lewis for REM, Austin, TX, 1985.

Los Cuatro. Editor & co-author, Barrio Publications, Denver, CO, 1971.

Obras. Quetzal-Vihio Press, Pembroke, NC, 1971.

Mano a Mano: Juan Contreras y Ricardo Sánchez. Conferencia de Unidad y Acción, n.p., n.d., El Paso, TX.

Film

Entelequia: An Original Screenplay. Chispa Productions, and University of Utah, Salt Lake City, UT, 1978.

■

Book design is by Vicki Trego Hill
of El Paso, Texas.

Cover illustration is by Jesus "Chista" Cantu
of San Antonio, Texas.

Photograph by Rikárd-Sergei Sánchez
of Albany, California.

Glossnotes® by M.S. Hetherington
of San Antonio, Texas.

The text typeface is Garamond and is set by
Camille of El Paso, Texas.

The book is printed by
McNaughton & Gunn, Inc. of Ann Arbor, Michigan.

EL PASO ■ TEXAS